Love Letters from Heaven

Praise for *Love Letters from Heaven*

"Your story is inspiring, meaningful, and powerful."—Muriel K.

"I felt such peace after reading *Love Letters from Heaven* that it has become my middle-of-the-night read! It calms me in a way that is very beautiful."—Elizabeth H.

"Quite simply, your story touched me with healing and grace."—Alma S.

"One cannot read *Love Letters from Heaven* without weeping a little. I like your crisp Hemingway-like writing style."—Monty D.

"Wow, you are a powerful storyteller! I read *Love Letters from Heaven* in one sitting. I am not religious in the Christian sense, either."—Jack P.

"Your story has 'legs.' I have shared it with several people who have benefited from your collaboration with Susan. It is a durable and energizing story."—Sam A.

"I am mailing three of your books to family members who I feel will benefit the most from your beautiful story of spiritual healing and awakening to the higher truths of life and death."—Sandy H.

"Your book is awesome. It's such a huge gift in all ways. Your story, Susan's story, your ability to tell it, and always with just the right words. You write with grace and conviction and marvelously well! What meant the most to me was how you came to believe in the resurrection. You present it all very simply in chapter twelve. It is clear, and it is convincing, and very, very moving."—Jean G.

"You write very well, and the story is a very compelling one. I continue to be moved each time I read it. I have been quite involved with Hospice and am trying to start a Hospice Volunteer Training Program for inmates in our local prison. It occurs to me that Hospice training should include more information on ADCs and try to normalize the phenomena, which would encourage more people to talk about their experiences. I would like to use your experience in the bereavement group I run at the prison."—Diane S.

The testimonials above are in response to an earlier limited and private printing by the author. This book contains previous material as well as new and revised material.

Love Letters from Heaven

After-Death Communication

and a Wife's Eternal Love

Morey McDaniel

iUniverse, Inc.
New York Bloomington

Love Letters from Heaven
After-Death Communication and a Wife's Eternal Love

iUniverse books may be ordered through booksellers or by contacting:

iUniverse
1663 Liberty Drive
Bloomington, IN 47403
www.iuniverse.com
1-800-Authors (1-800-288-4677)

ISBN: 978-1-4401-5713-4 (pbk)
ISBN: 978-1-4401-5714-1 (ebk)

Library of Congress Control Number: 2009932391

Printed in the United States of America

iUniverse rev. date: 09/08/2009

Contents

Acknowledgments

My special thanks to Rev. Harold E. "Skip" Masback, III, Rev. Lidabell Lunt Pollard, and Anne Engen for their support and encouragement in the weeks before and after Susan's death. You were my family.

My special thanks also to Rev. Charles Crawford Smith for leading the way by sharing with the congregation his experience of an after-death contact from a deceased friend.

My thanks to the many friends of Susan's and mine and to members of the Congregational Church in New Canaan, Connecticut, for their support and encouragement. You were our anchor.

My thanks also to Jeanne Fredericks, a literary agent, for her faith in my book; to Donna Gann, Charles Hedrick, Allan Young, and James Kellett for helpful comments; and to George Joslin and Laurel Robinson for editing my manuscript.

Most of all, my heartfelt thanks to you, Susan, for your love letters from heaven, the most wonderful gift of my life.

For Susan, the love of my life

Susan was strong, and she was brave,
and she died as she lived, brave to the end.

Preface

Love Letters from Heaven is a true story of life after death by a skeptical corporate lawyer who loses his wife Susan to cancer. He tells about the many surprising signs that came to him and several others after her death—signs that came as startling coincidences so numerous and ingenious one might call it super-synchronicity. Signs so moving and convincing that his faith is restored, his life transformed.

Significantly, a prominent New England church that traces its history back to the Puritans and the Pilgrims plays a major role, as do three senior ministers. The church itself is a setting for the story because it was in the sanctuary that the first sign appears to the author with a minister for a witness. The divine source of the signs is made explicit. They come from God and Jesus, and the signs bear messages from one or more of Susan, God, and Jesus.

It is no accident that a church, three of its ministers, and the sanctuary itself figure in these events. Even so, most after-death contacts are without religious content. With or without such content, all after-death contacts are relevant for everyone because they point to a transcendent reality.

Signs are symbolic. They have to be interpreted and decoded. In the Notes and Commentary, a number of the signs and symbols are explained more fully. The signs contain symbols of ancient origin and meaning.

Many people believe meaningful coincidences are divine messages. Others think such coincidences are meaningless random events. In the Afterword, this debate is put in sharper focus. Some coincidences may happen by accident, but others happen by design.

In an important first, after-death contacts coming directly and spontaneously from deceased loved ones are shown to have a biblical basis and to fulfill biblical promises. Such contacts are gifts from God to reassure us that there is life after death and that our deceased loved ones are alive and in heaven. They bring divine comfort and healing to those who grieve.

Introduction

In the summer of 1961, while we were on our honeymoon driving to California so I could start law school, I asked Susan, "Did you ever imagine what kind of man you would marry?"

"I thought I would marry a missionary, and we would go to Africa."

I laughed. She was getting a lawyer. Years later, I did become a missionary, but not as Susan envisioned.

There's a nickname for the Congregational Church: the "Congo" church. So, for a little while, you could say I was a missionary in a Congo church. My mission? To tell the story you are about to read. My mission continues, but to a wider audience.

Every Easter we celebrate the good news of Jesus' resurrection. But he was a unique figure, the son of God. What about the rest of us who are not so special? We all know about God's promise of eternal life. We hear about it at Easter and at funeral and memorial services. But that promise was made nearly two thousand years ago in a time and place even Bible scholars only dimly understand. It's hard for some of us to believe a promise like that, much as we may want to.

I'm from Missouri, the "Show-Me" State. I want

God to show me some evidence that he has made good on his promise to someone like us. And he did show me. That's what my story is about: a promise made good. It's a contemporary resurrection story, the good news for the rest of us.

On July 12, 2000, almost a month after our thirty-ninth wedding anniversary, Susan died from ovarian cancer. She was sixty-one. Ten days after she died, there began a series of remarkable signs. They came one after another, building on each other, reinforcing each other, culminating in the most profound experience of my life.

There are all kinds and varieties of religious and spiritual experiences. The ones I've had are frequently called "after-death communications," or ADCs for short. They are a direct and spontaneous experience.

Direct because the ADC comes to you without the use of an intermediary, such as a medium, psychic, hypnotist, or therapist, and without the use of a technique, ritual, apparatus, or device, such as gazing, a séance, ouija board, crystal ball, mirrors, or the like.

Spontaneous because the ADC is not initiated or induced. The source, not the recipient, determines when, where, and how the ADC takes place. ADCs happen suddenly and without warning, taking you by surprise. Their duration is usually brief but is always breathtaking. The immediate source for most ADCs is a deceased family member or friend. Sometimes it is a divine figure (God, Jesus, an angel), and sometimes it is both. The ultimate source for all comforting ADCs is God.

ADCs are more common than people think. Based on their seven years of research and interviews of 2000 people of diverse backgrounds, Bill and Judy Guggenheim, authors of *Hello from Heaven!,* estimate that at least 20 percent of the population of the United States has had one or more after-death communications. At the present time, that's 60 million Americans. Numbers of such magnitude demonstrate that ADCs are an extremely common human experience.

On April 23, 2001, I told my story to the public for the first time in a program, "Life after Life: Love Letters from Heaven," at the Congregational Church in New Canaan, Connecticut. This book emerged from that program.

On October 22, 2001, I conducted a second program at the church, "Life after Life: Signs and Visitors from Heaven." Five ADC stories were told, two from former senior ministers of the church, and three from members of the church, including me. At the close of the program, I asked for a show of hands from those who believed they had received an after-death contact from a deceased loved one. At least three-quarters of the audience raised their hands, a cloud of witnesses.

On December 8, 2002, I conducted a third program at a sister church, the Saugatuck Congregational Church in Westport, Connecticut. Again, five ADC stories were told, including two from members of that church. Again, I asked for a show of hands from those who believed they had been contacted by a deceased loved one. Again, at least three-quarters of the audience raised their hands, another cloud of witnesses. People with ADC experiences are all around us. They are everywhere. It is one of the best-kept secrets in America.

ADCs come in three basic kinds: sensory experiences, dreams, and symbolic signs. A sensory experience might be a vision or apparition you see, a voice you hear, a touch you feel, a fragrance you smell, a sense of the deceased's presence, or a combination of two or more of those sensations. Dreams of visitation are clear, vivid, and intense. They seem so real they feel like they are actually happening, and they are easily remembered.

My experiences were of the third kind, symbolic signs in the form of coincidences. I think I know why. If I had seen an apparition or heard a voice, I would have dismissed it as a hallucination, my mind playing tricks on me because of my grief. Likewise, I would have discounted any unusual dream as grief-induced.

I am not a person prone to believing in things like ADCs. I am a retired corporate lawyer. I graduated from Wesleyan University and earned my law degree from Stanford Law School and an advanced law degree from Harvard Law School. For twenty years, I was chief finance counsel in the law department of a large industrial corporation headquartered in New York City, and later in Connecticut. I am by nature a skeptic made worse by my legal training. For a while, in the months before Susan's death, I became so skeptical and doubtful that I lost my faith entirely.

My ADC experiences had three principal features. First, there were multiple signs; second, the divine source of the signs was made explicit; and third, every sign I received had a witness in addition to me or has documentary support. In a few cases, someone else received a sign and reported it to me. You could tell this story without me. In legal terms, I have corroborative evidence for all the signs.

Why so elaborate a series of signs? Probably because they were designed for a skeptic of the worst kind, a lawyer like me. The signs also have a personal touch. They were designed for someone who loves books and wordplay, namely me. An intelligent designer was at work, for the signs are inventive and clever. In time, I came to see that the signs, although serious beyond measure, are lighthearted and sweet, even playful, as if coming from a good-natured soul, which they did.

The Gospel continues to be written in the stories of our lives. Sadly, we hide our stories from each other for a variety of reasons:

People might think we are mentally disturbed. We might be criticized or ridiculed. It's too personal to share. Sharing it would dilute the experience and cheapen it. Because not everyone gets a sign, sharing it might make others in the family jealous and make friends and others feel inadequate. People won't believe us. They won't understand. And so on.

By telling my story, I want to encourage others to step forward and share their stories. Maybe then, after-death communications and other religious and spiritual experiences will become normal and acceptable subjects of everyday conversation, in church and out of church, bringing hope and reassurance to all.

1. Before Susan's Death

My story begins on Sunday, November 1, 1998. On that day, Susan is diagnosed with Stage Four ovarian cancer, the most advanced stage. On average, out of each hundred women with that diagnosis, only one to five of them will be alive five years later. Susan's diagnosis amounts to a probable death sentence. A week later, Susan is admitted to Memorial Sloan-Kettering Hospital in New York City, a leading hospital for cancer treatment.

Tuesday, November 10. Dressed in a simple hospital gown, Susan takes her IV pole in hand and pushes it along as we walk down the hall from her room to the patient lounge. There we can talk without disturbing Susan's roommate. It is late in the evening. The lounge is empty. We are alone. Her surgery is scheduled for the next day.

Susan is excited, like a child about to embark on the biggest adventure of her life. Her cheeks are flushed; a radiance is on her face. She has a strange beauty about her. Where have I seen this before? Of course—in old paintings by the masters of the Virgin Mary and other women Saints. With sadness in my heart, I catch a glimpse of Susan's destiny. She has been called away to join all the saints in heaven, and nothing in this world will change that. Tears well up in my eyes. I tell no one.

The next day Susan undergoes major surgery and is in the operating room for more than three hours. The surgery is only partially successful. Over the next sixteen months, Susan will try seven different chemotherapy treatments. Although two or three buy her some time, ultimately they all fail.

Wednesday, March 8, 2000. Susan and I meet with her oncologist. The latest chemotherapy drug, Gemzar, Susan's last best hope, has failed. Debilitated by five weeks of nausea from the Gemzar, Susan tells her doctor she has had enough and wants to stop the treatments. He agrees. The next day hospice steps in and takes over.

Soon after, on a day in March, I encounter Anne Engen, a neighbor, on my daily walk around a two-mile circle near my house. I stop to talk with her as I always do. I am in miserable shape. Susan's approaching death has put my belief in an afterlife to the test, and I've failed it. I simply do not believe the resurrection stories in the Bible. Here I am, about to lose my wife, and I have lost my faith. I am in tears.

Anne quietly asks me, "Have you heard of ADCs?" All I can think of is *Aid to Dependent Children.*

"No, I haven't."

ADCs, she explains, are after-death communications. She tells me about a book with that title. I am polite but skeptical.

Then Anne does something remarkable. She tells me

about an ADC experience her sister-in-law had. Anne is a trustee of the church. She's a sane and sensible person. It is a magic moment for me. For the first time, I get a glimmer of hope that maybe death is not the final chapter after all.

I order the book, *After-Death Communication*, from Amazon. The author, Louis LaGrand, is a certified grief counselor and former college professor. His book is a helpful and knowledgeable work. So I order his second book on ADCs, *Messages and Miracles.*

Not long after, on a day in April, Rev. Lidabell Pollard, the senior minister at our church, makes one of her weekly pastoral visits to our house. Susan is now a terminal cancer patient, and we need all the counseling and support we can get. I admire Lidabell's grace and compassion in talking with a woman who will soon die. I want to ask her about ADCs, but I hesitate, unsure if this is a proper topic to take up with a minister.

Finally, I get up my nerve and say, "I've been reading this book Anne Engen told me about on after-death communications ..." Before I can say another word, Lidabell turns to me and says, "Oh, those happen all the time."

I breathe a sigh of relief.

She then tells Susan and me about Rev. Charles Smith, the senior minister who preceded her. Charlie had a wonderful ADC experience as a young seminary student. Many years later, he got up in the pulpit and told the entire congregation about it on an Easter

Sunday. I sit spellbound as Lidabell tells us Charlie's story, retold here in his own words:

"In the spring of 1953, I went to Glover, a small town in Vermont, to begin my duties as a student summer minister at the Congregational church. The day I arrived I met Pearl Drew, a retired dairy farmer who lived across the street from the house where I was staying. During the next four months, we became fast friends. Evenings, we discussed topics close to his heart: sports, politics, automobiles, hunting and fishing, guns, bows and arrows—and the life to come.

"Pearly was devoted to his wife who had died three years earlier. Was she in heaven? What is heaven? Where is heaven, and what is it like? How do you get there? How will we recognize loved ones if there is a life to come?

"I did my best responding to his heartfelt concerns. We talked about how Jesus appeared to those who knew him and loved him, and how they recognized him. We talked about living on after death and concluded that, if we do, our personalities are not destroyed. They retain their integrity, they can be recognized, and we will be reunited with those we love by ties of the spirit.

"Many times I joked with him saying, 'Pearl, if you get there before I do, come back and tell me about it.' Upon leaving Glover at the end of the summer of 1953, I never saw Pearl Drew in this life again. He died not long after I left.

"Two years later, in 1955, driving a very used Oldsmobile I found for a hundred dollars, I stopped on a lonely stretch of the Fall River expressway to add oil to my engine, a process that had to be repeated every fifty miles. It was two o'clock on a fall Friday afternoon.

"I was now working at the First Congregational Church of Fall River, Massachusetts. Many in my congregation had the same questions that Pearl Drew had. While I was pouring oil into my engine, I was thinking about Pearly and what I was telling my congregation about life and death, when I looked up.

"There was Pearly standing beside me. He was as real and alive to me as you are. Wearing his same old faded dark green work shirt, pants, and matching cap, his face beaming with a big grin, he said, 'Charles, we never knew the half of it.' Then he vanished."

I'm amazed to hear all this. Lidabell is a much loved and respected senior minister of a mainline church in this affluent and conservative town of New Canaan, and she's telling me that ADCs "happen all the time." Moreover, her predecessor experienced a dramatic ADC and told the congregation about it on an Easter Sunday.

I am feeling like the proverbial kid who is always the last one on the block to get the word. My faith starts to come back, but from a direction I never could have imagined. I get bolder. At least three times in May, I ask Susan to send me a message from the other side that she's okay. "But Susan, don't scare me." The last time I bring it up she says matter-of-factly, "I'll do it." She speaks in a strange voice with such quiet authority that I'm taken aback. I never mention it again.

Wednesday, May 31. Susan goes into Stamford Hospital for minor surgery. When the surgeon makes the incision, he discovers so much cancer in her abdomen that he is unable to perform the operation. Susan remains in the hospital and never comes home again.

Thursday, July 6. Rev. Skip Masback, the associate minister, visits Susan and me at the hospital in the evening. While there, he prays for me that I might have a "foretaste of things to come"—in other words, a sign from Susan after her death that there is life after life. It is the last time Skip will see Susan alive.

Wednesday, July 12, 2000. Susan dies in her sleep at five o'clock in the morning. In her last days on earth, the cancer has laid waste her body, and she looks like a Holocaust victim with the face of death even in life.

2. A Sparrow

Although Susan dies in July, her memorial service is postponed until September because so many people are away on vacation. In May, Susan selected some of the music she wants for her service. She picked "His Eye Is on the Sparrow" as one of her favorites.

July 22, ten days after Susan dies. I meet with Skip Saturday morning in the church library. I show him a draft of the proposed order of service. He glances at it and puts it aside. He spends an hour or so with me. As our conversation draws to a close, he says, "Let's go down to the sanctuary and pray." That seems a bit formal to me, but I follow him downstairs. He unlocks the sanctuary, and we sit side by side in the front pew.

Skip begins to pray for me. All of a sudden, from the back of the sanctuary, a creature of some sort starts making a racket. The noisy disturbance comes in bursts, and then it's quiet again. Skip tries to ignore the interruptions, but he can't. He gives up and says, "We have to do something about this."

We walk to the back of the sanctuary; Skip takes one aisle, and I take the other. As I near the back of the sanctuary, a bird flies out from behind a large window shade, streaks over my right shoulder, heads straight toward the window in front of me, and lights on it.

I yell over to Skip, "It's a sparrow." I stand still and watch the sparrow, quiet now, its feet grasping a window mullion, its wings spread across the pane. As I stare at the sparrow, I say to myself, *You're a plump, healthy-looking bird*. Then it flies off again.

I climb up to the balcony to help Skip open windows to give the bird an avenue of escape. The seconds tick by. Suddenly, my mind begins to reel. The song, the song about the sparrow, I can't remember the title. In a panic, I struggle to remember. Finally, the words come to me, "His eye is on the sparrow, and I know He watches me." Then it hits me. The sparrow is a symbol for Susan, and the words of the song are a message from Susan.

She is saying, "His eye, Morey's eye, is on the sparrow, and I know he watches me." My eye was on the sparrow, and I was watching her. In an instant, I know Susan is alive and well and in another place. That's not all I know, either. The sparrow appeared to me in the sanctuary, the most holy place in this Christian church, with a minister for a witness. I know who sent the sparrow. I burst into tears, tears of joy. I point out to Skip the connection between the sparrow and the song.

"Yes, I know," he replies. "I saw the song in the draft you handed me earlier." Skip is wise enough and kind enough to let his slower-witted friend make the connection for himself. After the sparrow zips out a window we've opened, Skip locates the place where it got in. The church exterior is being painted, and a painter failed to close one window completely. There is a two-inch crack the bird slipped through.

"I've been here seven and a half years," says Skip, "and I have never seen or heard of any bird getting in this sanctuary before." By this time, the full import of the sparrow's appearance is beginning to sink in with Skip and me.

"Do you realize," he says, "the celestial mechanics that had to be lined up for this to happen?"

It was true. If it had not been the summer the church was being painted, if the painter had not left a small opening in one window the day before, if Skip had not come home from vacation for a few days for some family matters, if he had not taken time from his busy schedule to invite me over to the church to meet with him, if we had not met at the time we did on Saturday morning, if Skip had not taken me down to the sanctuary, nothing would have happened. Skip and I return to the front pew and sit down again.

Skip starts to pray. "Ten minutes ago, this would have been a different prayer," he says. I don't remember anything else Skip said. I keep repeating over and over in my mind, *My eye was on the sparrow, and she knew I was watching her.* Later, I remember my first words when I was staring at the sparrow. *You're a plump, healthy-looking bird.* I realize then that Susan has been made whole.

I also realize the sparrow could not have been in the sanctuary much before we came in. The sparrow flew out from behind the window shade of the same window that was left open. If the sparrow had been there much longer, it probably would have been loose inside the sanctuary. The sparrow did not know, and I did not know, that we had a date with destiny.

The next day, Sunday, July 23. I meet with Lidabell in her office after the morning service. I tell her what happened in the sanctuary the day before. When I mention that the messenger was a sparrow, Lidabell exclaims, "Oh, that's so like Susan!" In the Bible, she points out, the sparrow is an ordinary, common bird. Susan was so humble and modest that it would be like her, says Lidabell, to have a sparrow represent her.

It's true. Susan was a plain woman with a natural and wholesome beauty. Practical, thrifty, and down-to-earth, she had little interest in clothes, cosmetics, hairdos, and jewelry. She loved gardening and the outdoors. Low-key and reserved, she did not like to attract attention or to stand out from the crowd. Somewhat shy, she just wanted to be one of the flock.

I mention to Lidabell that Skip had never heard of a bird getting into the sanctuary before.

"I've served this church nineteen years," says Lidabell, "and we've never had a bird in the sanctuary before. We've had mice, bees, and a few other creatures, but no birds."

Soon after the sparrow's appearance, I take another look at the two ADC books by Louis LaGrand to see what they have to say about birds as signs. In the back of both books is a suggested reading list. I had looked at the two lists once before when Susan was still alive. I glance at the two lists again. After what happened in the sanctuary, a book on one of the lists leaps off the page:

S. Sparrow, *I Am With You Always*

I stare at the title and the author's name for a long time. Sparrow is an unusual last name. S. is the initial of Susan's first name. What a sweet message, "I am with you always." To my further surprise, I find this message in a book appropriately titled

Messages and Miracles

I visit Amazon to find out more about the book *I Am With You Always*. The subtitle of the book turns out to be:

True Stories of Encounters with Jesus

There is a larger message for me now. My encounter with the sparrow in the sanctuary was, indeed, an encounter with a messenger from Jesus, and the message from him, and the message from Susan, is the same: "I am with you always."

3. Another Sparrow

Thursday, August 10. Six of Susan's prep school classmates who live in Maine get together for their annual luncheon and mini-reunion. They meet at Ann Waldron's home. Ann takes her five guests to the Rockefeller Gardens on Mount Desert Island. A year earlier, Ann took Susan to those same gardens, which are near Acadia National Park.

When the six women arrive at the gardens, Ann hears and recognizes the song of one of her favorite songbirds. After touring the gardens, the women hold an observance there for Susan. In a quiet place shaded by trees, they form a circle and join hands. Each in turn says a few words about Susan and what she meant to them. When it's Ann's turn, she observes the moment in silence. The silence is broken when the bird sings again, the second and only other time its song is heard.

I call Ann that evening. She tells me about the observance for Susan. Three times I have to ask her, "What kind of bird was it?" Three times she tells me. I can't believe what I'm hearing. It was a white-throated sparrow. Ann does not know about the sparrow in the sanctuary. So I tell her what happened there. Like me, she is astonished.

By this time, I have obtained all the words to "His Eye Is on the Sparrow." The connection between the song and the sparrow in the sanctuary makes me wonder if there also is a connection between the song and this second sparrow in Maine. The song has a four-line chorus. The first sparrow gave a special meaning to the last two lines of the chorus:

His eye is on the sparrow,
and I know He watches me.

With the song sparrow in mind, I take a look at the first two lines of the chorus:

I sing because I'm happy,
I sing because I'm free.

Amazing! The words fit. A singing sparrow brings another message from Susan. She sings because she's happy, she sings because she's free. Free of a body ravaged by cancer, free of cares and worries, free as a bird in the air. Two sparrows have translated the four-line chorus into a special message from heaven. I remember something Susan said to me several weeks before she died: *There are other worlds to sing in*, a strange and beautiful premonition of things to come.

Later, I write up the story of the song sparrow in Maine. When I write that the bird "sings again," I misspell *sings*. I overlook my error at first because I write another word with the same five letters. Surprisingly, both words fit the sentence. The other word is *signs*, an anagram of *sings*. When the sparrow was singing, it also was signing, in case I had any doubts.

4. A Fireball

Saturday, August 12, two days after the sparrow in Maine. I visit Alice Vining at her summer home in Vermont. Alice is a friend and classmate of Susan's from her prep school days. It is a weekend in August during the annual Perseid meteor showers. After dinner at Alice's, five of us go out to a meadow to look for shooting stars. We are there less than twenty minutes when I see a spectacular shooting star, unlike any I've ever seen.

It is very low in the sky as it travels parallel to the ground, streaking across the sky from my left to my right just above a small ridge opposite me. I stand there transfixed. I've never seen a shooting star at such close range. The white tail is short and stubby with a fiery orange tinge. It appears out of nowhere and vanishes in three seconds or less, making no sound at all.

At first, I'm not sure what it is. Maybe it's some kind of fireworks display. After it's gone, I realize it was the real thing. Of the five of us standing in the meadow, only one other person sees it; the rest are looking in the wrong direction.

Is it another sign? I don't know. If it is, the only message I can think of is *Expect the unexpected.* That's not good enough. I decide it is not a sign, just an astronomical curiosity. Three weeks later, another sign causes me to change my mind about the fiery meteor in Vermont. Still later, I learn the meteor was an unusual kind seldom seen.

It was a "fireball."

5. A Hawk

Tuesday, September 5, eleven days before Susan's memorial service. I am on the phone talking to my sister, Marianne. It's two forty-five in the afternoon. I'm standing in the kitchen facing the far wall as I talk. I turn to look outdoors. Perched on my deck railing not twenty feet away is a hawk looking in my direction.

"Wow, you're beautiful!" I cry out. The hawk is a beautiful creamy white and reddish brown. I tell Marianne over the phone what's happening. I stand there right in front of the sliding glass doors in full view of the hawk, looking at it while it looks at me. At the same time, I continue my live-action reporting to Marianne direct from the scene.

This is very strange behavior for a wild hawk. I've never seen one come so close. Surely, it must see me, notwithstanding the reflections on the glass. After all, hawks are known for their keen eyesight. After three or four minutes, the hawk departs in a leisurely fashion. I step out onto the deck and stand where the hawk was. I find I can see through the reflections on the glass, although barely. So the hawk definitely saw me. From a bird book, I determine that it was a red-tailed hawk.

Is this another sign? But what does it mean? This

is a sparrow story, not a hawk story. Then I remember what I said when I first saw the hawk, and I understand. Susan is not a sparrow anymore. She's like the hawk, beautiful and graceful, and she soars in the heavens. I get choked up. I can't talk anymore. I tell Marianne I will have to call her back.

A day or so later, I call Sandy Haviland, a friend of Susan's, and tell her about the hawk. She in turn tells me, "Morey, Native Americans believe that when a hawk lands near you, it bears a message from God." For a moment, I'm speechless.

"Sandy, how do you know that?"

"It's in a book I have."

Then I remember the blazing meteor that streaked across the Vermont sky and the only message that came to mind: *Expect the unexpected.* The hawk certainly was unexpected, and if the hawk is a messenger from God, the meteor takes on a new relevance.

It appears that God himself, creator of the cosmos, is announcing his presence, not with a burning bush, but with a burning meteor, a celestial shot fired across my bow. The meteor was an impressive display of firepower, and it left me in a state of awe. It also was a not-so-subtle reminder that he who can send harmless little sparrows on errands also can hurl fireballs across the sky.

Friday, September 8, three days after the hawk visits me. I find Skip in his office and tell him about the hawk.

"Whoa, this is heavy duty," he says. He then teaches me things I did not expect to learn. About a church youth group mission trip to Arizona to help a Hopi tribe repair some of their homes and buildings. About Hopi religious beliefs and practices. About remarkable parallels between their religion and Christianity.

Skip sums it up this way: "Just as Christ is the intermediary between God and Christians, the eagle is the intermediary between the Great Spirit and the tribe. Whenever Hopis participate in a religious dance or ritual, they always have an eagle feather in their hand."

"What about hawks?"

"Same thing—they are akin to eagles. I once had a farm in West Virginia. Hawks used to circle in the sky everyday. I never came closer than a thousand feet to one of them."

The next day I get an e-mail from Sandy confirming what Skip has said about hawks being akin to eagles. Sandy has a book by an Oglala Sioux lawyer who writes, "The red-tailed hawk is a messenger. It is close to the eagle, and its gifts are very similar to those of its larger flying relative."

Two different sources, Sandy and Skip, are both telling me the same thing. The hawk who visited me was a messenger from God. Although most red-tailed hawks have a band of spots on their chest, some do not. The one I saw did not. It was "spotless," as befits a heavenly messenger.

It's curious that Native American religious symbols, beliefs, and practices are becoming part of this story, but I am not surprised. Susan was not an indoor person. In addition to her passion for gardening, Susan enjoyed the challenge and thrill of outdoor adventure. A little danger only made it more exciting. Although a small woman, she was strong and athletic. She loved hiking, camping, canoeing, kayaking, sailing, swimming, and horseback riding. Her two favorite vacation destinations were the Rocky Mountain West and the Atlantic Ocean shoreline.

Susan's idol was Sacagawea, the young Shoshone woman who served as a guide and interpreter for Meriwether Lewis and William Clark on their famous expedition to explore the Pacific Northwest. Susan admired Sacagawea and envied her having the opportunity to accompany the Corps of Discovery on their path-breaking explorations.

Now Susan, as my Sacagawea, is guiding me on the most extraordinary journey of my life, a journey in this world following a trail marked with signs from out of this world.

6. A Hawk Feather

Sunday, September 10, six days before Susan's memorial service. I attend the nine-thirty morning church service. Afterward, Anne Engen sees me and comes over to talk to me. I tell her about the hawk. Later in the day around three o'clock, there's a knock at my door. It's Anne. She has a feather in her hand.

"When I was taking my walk around the circle today, I found this hawk feather, and I want you to have it." She hands me the feather and explains why she is pretty sure it is a hawk feather.

Not five hours have passed since I told Anne about the hawk, and she "happens" to find a hawk feather along the road. Hawk feathers are not a common sight. A hawk feather is a rare find, and people who know what a hawk feather looks like also are a rare find.

"Anne, do you know the religious significance of hawk and eagle feathers for Native Americans?"

"Only that they are a big deal."

So I tell her what Skip told me two days ago and explain the significance of her gift to me. "When you arrived at my door, you had a hawk feather in your hand. You gave it to me, and now I hold it in my hand. Today is Sunday, a day of religious observance for Christians.

With this feather, like a Hopi brave in a religious dance, I am more than an observer, I am a participant in this unfolding story." Later, I put the feather in a glass and set it on the fireplace mantel as a daily reminder of my role in this strange and beautiful adventure.

7. Another Hawk

Monday, September 11, five days before Susan's memorial service. I call my sister, Marianne, who lives in a suburb of St. Louis, Missouri. I tell her about Anne's gift to me of a hawk feather the day before. With this piece of information, Marianne knows all the major elements of the story: the two sparrows, the fireball, the hawk, the hawk feather.

About twenty minutes after we talk on the phone, Marianne walks into her home office, which has a large picture window with a view of the backyard. She sits down at her desk and looks out the window. Perched on a nearby tree limb about sixty feet away is a hawk facing in her direction. Marianne has lived in her house for six years and never seen a hawk anywhere in her neighborhood. Puzzled, she calls me back and asks, "What do you think it means?"

"I think all the messages I've received are meant for you as well."

For twenty months, from November 1998, when Susan was in the hospital recovering from surgery, until July 2000, when she died, Marianne sent Susan a card or a note every day. If a day was missed, the next day she sent two. In the Spring of 1999, Marianne took Susan to

Eureka Springs, Arkansas, for several days, a place that Marianne calls her "power place," a place of healing.

In early June of 2000, shortly after Susan went into the hospital, never to return home again, Marianne made a special trip, traveling alone from St. Louis, to New York City, and on to New Canaan, to visit Susan in the hospital for several days. No one else, family or friends, traveled so far just to call on Susan in the hospital.

This second hawk, it appears, is a thank-you from Susan to Marianne via God for her caring and concern. And by it, brother and sister are made joint heirs to an incredible legacy from Susan.

8. Another Hawk Feather

Soon after Anne gives me the hawk feather, her sister-in-law suggests that the hawk feather Anne found was a thank-you from Susan to Anne. I don't think so. I still think it is a message to me that I am a participant now, and not just a spectator.

Saturday, September 16. It is the day of Susan's memorial service. Susan was active in the women's garden club, helped at the nature center, and served in the volunteer ambulance corps as an emergency medical technician (EMT). A lot of people knew Susan, and many attend the service—so many that the sanctuary is near capacity.

A vocalist opens the service with "His Eye Is on the Sparrow." Later in the service she sings "On Eagle's Wings," a piece Lidabell selected with unknowing foresight in July *before* any of the signs occurred. Skip and Lidabell jointly conduct the service.

Members of the ambulance corps attend in full dress uniform and sit together in pews roped off for them, serving as an unofficial honor guard. During the service, they are asked to stand and be recognized. It is a powerful and moving moment as they rise together to honor one of their own. Tears run down my cheeks. It is a beautiful service for a beautiful person. At the close of the service, a member of the church is overheard saying to his wife, "That's the service I want."

Sunday, September 17, the day after the memorial service. Early in the morning, Anne Engen's husband takes one of Anne's little corgi dogs for a walk. He and the little dog find a hawk feather in their front yard and take it to Anne. This feather, for sure, is Susan's thank-you to Anne. Anne's sister-in-law was prescient. Anne would receive a thank-you feather from Susan, but it would come the following Sunday.

9. A Minister

Tuesday, September 19, three days after the memorial service. I drive to a beautiful sandy beach on the south shore of eastern Long Island near Montauk, New York. Susan's sister, Cindy, and my sister, Marianne, are with me. The three of us have gone there to pour Susan's ashes into the Atlantic Ocean. The beach is not too distant from the Village of Westhampton Beach, where Susan spent many happy summer days in her youth, and where she grew to be a strong and graceful swimmer, a seaworthy sailor, and an accomplished equestrian.

The summer season is over, and the beach is empty. It's a clear and sunny day with a chill in the air and a brisk wind. Standing near the water's edge, Cindy and I read a prayer Susan once wrote for her mother when her mother's ashes were poured into the ocean. Then I wade out into the water and pour Susan's ashes into the ocean, the ocean she grew up with, the ocean she loved.

That night a storm rolls in. While I'm driving to dinner in heavy rain, strong winds pepper my car and windshield with sand blowing off the dunes. As the wipers beat back and forth, sand gets caught in them, and my windshield is scratched up. When I get home,

I call an auto glass shop to have them replace my windshield. To my surprise, they make house calls.

Thursday, September 28. The windshield installer drives up to my house. I am waiting for him in my driveway. He jumps out of his truck and cheerfully greets me, "Hi, I'm Kevin. How are you today?"

For some reason, to this total stranger, I tell the truth, "Not so well. I've lost my wife …" I break into tears.

Kevin approaches me, puts an arm around my shoulders, and says, "You know, I'm going to quit this job soon. I'm training to be a minister. May I pray for you?"

I nod and he does just that. He prays for me. I don't hear much of what Kevin says because I am too overcome with emotion by the startling discovery he is a minister. I am in pain, and God in his mercy sends a minister, a real one, disguised as a mechanic, to comfort me in the middle of my own driveway.

Kevin then turns to the work at hand and in short order replaces my windshield with a new one. I get in the car to check it out. "Yes, I can see clearly now." I was not referring to the windshield.

10. Follow Your Bliss

A few weeks later, it occurs to me that the "Sparrow" might have another message for me at Amazon. So I do a book search. For author, I type in "Sparrow," nothing else. Quite a few books come up, but one stands out:

Susan Sparrow, *Follow Your Bliss*

Most book listings on Amazon include an image of the book's cover. At that time, this listing did not. I order the book. When it arrives, I make a surprising discovery. On the cover of the book is a magnificent hawk soaring in a sunset sky.

Susan, the sparrow, and the hawk—or in symbolic terms, Susan, Jesus, and God—are telling me, "Follow your bliss," a famous line of Joseph Campbell's, the great mythologist. It means: "Seek out in life what gives you deep joy, your true calling, your soul's delight."

Like other signs, this sign also bears more than one message. In effect, Susan, Jesus, and God also are telling me, "We care about you, we love you, we want the best for you."

11. A Third Hawk, a Third Sparrow

Easter Sunday, April 15, 2001. It is my first Easter without Susan. I get in my car to drive to church. I turn on the radio to a classical music station. The first sound I hear is not music. The first thing to come out of the radio is a man's voice and these words: "I am with you always," the words of Jesus spoken to me. What a timely and reassuring greeting on this Easter morning!

Monday, April 23, eight days after Easter. As mentioned earlier, on this date I told the foregoing story to the public for the first time in a program, "Life after Life: Love Letters from Heaven," at the Congregational Church in New Canaan, Connecticut. What was not mentioned is this: The turnout is unexpectedly large, 150–200 people. I am surprised by the turnout, but not nearly as surprised as the church's three ministers, who are astonished. So many come that the event is moved from the parlor to the sanctuary, the largest space in the church and, fittingly enough, the place where the first sign appeared to Skip and me.

My talk is taped. At the end of May, I mail out nearly fifty audiotapes to friends, relatives, and others. I send one to my best friend and high-school classmate, Jim

Hurd, who lives in Springfield, Missouri, where I was born and grew up.

Although I told Jim some time ago that I had received a number of extraordinary signs after Susan's death, I did not reveal any details, uncertain as I am about the reaction of others. As soon as the tape arrives in the mail, Jim listens to it. He sends me an e-mail. This is what he told me:

"As I listened to your tape, I recalled some strange events in the same time frame. Late last summer, I heard a strange sound in my backyard just before dark. It sounded like a lamb in distress. The cry came and went for about half an hour, then stopped. I've never heard such a sound before or since.

"As you know, I have bird feeders and enjoy identifying my feathered friends. A few days later, I was visiting the Springfield Conservation Nature Center looking for books on Missouri birds. I spoke to a couple of Missouri conservation agents there and mentioned the sound I had heard in my backyard. They thought it might have been a screech owl and suggested I get an audiotape *Missouri Bird Calls*, which I did.

"Listening to the tape on my way home, I identified the sound I heard. It was a red-tailed hawk. Once you hear that cry, you will never forget it. Not long after that, I saw an unfamiliar bird at the feeder outside the window of my home office. It lingered long enough for me to consult my bird book. It was a white-throated sparrow. I have never seen another. I believe Susan sent me the hawk and the sparrow to remind me of the e-mail promise I made to her on her deathbed that I would always be there for you. After hearing your story, I have a renewed faith in how a greater power can work in our lives."

From Sandy Haviland, I first learn that hawks are seen as divine messengers by Native Americans. From her, I also learn about the book *Mother Earth Spirituality* by a Sioux lawyer. From his book, I learn about the special significance for the Sioux of a red-tailed hawk. As I am explaining this to Jim in an e-mail, I discover something I have overlooked for nine months. It's a pun, more wordplay for my amusement and enlightenment:

Sioux = Sue

Jim's red-tailed hawk was a "Sue" messenger. The one who visited me was my own "Sue" messenger. As an added touch, I, who was Sue's lawyer-husband, learn about red-tailed hawks from a Sioux lawyer.

The many signs add up to an imaginative and lighthearted little playlet, sophisticated in design, simple in content, and symbolic in form, a miniature allegory. The principal actors are "Susan" sparrows and "Sue" hawks, some from nature, some from books, with a fireball representing God's presence.

The allegory has two acts separated by an interlude. In the first act come "Susan" sparrows, messengers from Jesus. In the interlude, a fireball heralds more powerful signs to follow. In the second act comes the first "Sue" hawk, a majestic messenger from God. It all builds to a climax when Susan, a sparrow, and a hawk come on stage together and say in unison, "Follow your bliss!"

In the last weeks of her life, I asked Susan to send me a sign, but not to scare me. She said she would. She kept her word and more.

12. A Glimpse of God's Glory

Susan was my wife for thirty-nine years. Her death is the worst loss of my life. Yet the experiences that followed after her death were the greatest gift of my life, truly a glimpse of God's glory. From the valley of the shadow of death, I was catapulted to the mountain peak. It was crazy. Susan died, Susan lives. I was shedding tears of grief and joy all at the same time. The promise Jesus made in the Sermon on the Mount was fulfilled: "Blessed are those who mourn, for they will be comforted." I was comforted, and in extraordinary way.

The many signs I received were the most profound experience of my life, almost overwhelming, shaking me to my core. I had what theologians call a "numinous" experience, where one feels "undeniably, irresistibly, and unforgettably in the presence of the Divine."

The experience transformed my life. I no longer fear death. I am more spiritual, compassionate, and outgoing. I feel a sense of joy and peace. I am filled with gratitude for my life, for family and friends, for the awesome beauty of the world around us. The world is not the same for me anymore. It is an enchanted place filled with mystery and wonder.

The experience was so powerful and beautiful that

I felt called to share it with anyone who would listen. For I had good news, wonderful news, to tell. So I did tell my story, and it helped to heal me. In the process, I touched a number of lives and was doubly rewarded, for I who was comforted could now comfort others.

My faith was restored from unbelief to beyond belief to knowledge of the life to come. Before Susan died, I had read enough in and about the Bible to doubt the historical truth of many of the stories about Jesus. So I asked myself: What has to be historically true for me to believe?

My answer: Jesus lived, Jesus died, Jesus was resurrected. For me, as for the apostle Paul, everything turned on the resurrection. If Jesus was not raised from the dead, said Paul, our faith is futile.

There is historical evidence outside the Bible that Jesus lived and died. But I did not believe the stories in the Bible about Jesus' resurrection. For a while, I lost my faith, and with Susan's approaching death I was miserable. Then my world changed. Susan was raised from the dead. I found in the literature hundreds of accounts of modern-day ADC experiences. In addition, a number of people in my church told me about their ADC experiences, all of which helped to validate my own experience.

Since ADCs happen in such large numbers and with such regularity in our time, they must have happened in earlier times as well. So it became easy for me to believe that Jesus was raised from the dead and appeared to some of his followers. ADCs, I discovered, help to validate the central event of Christianity. Some may wonder how relevant Jesus' resurrection is for the rest of us since he was no ordinary mortal. Thanks to ADCs, we know that ordinary people are raised from the dead all the time.

Love, it seems, is the medium for ADC experiences. The one who dies contacts one or more of those he or she knew and loved in this life, such as a family member or friend. So it is with Jesus. In the Gospels, Jesus appears only to those he was close to and who loved him.

In summary, from my experience and the symbolism of the signs, I have learned these things:

1. Only an all-powerful, all-knowing, ever-present, loving Intelligence could send such signs. There is a God.
2. Susan is alive. There is life after death.
3. Susan is in another and better place. There is a heaven.
4. She is happy and healthy, beautiful and graceful.
5. Susan and Jesus are with me always.
6. Life and love are eternal.

These things are all so elementary, like a Sunday school lesson for small children, but with one enormous difference—God is my teacher.

I acquired my knowledge of the Divine at a very high cost—the loss of a much-loved wife. Although I am blessed to have this knowledge, and it reassures me and comforts me, it does not fill the hole in my heart. I miss Susan greatly. I will be glad to see her again.

Afterword

Science and Coincidence

Based on a materialistic conception of reality, science has its own explanations for coincidences and ADCs. Psychiatry has its views, too, views that might surprise you. In this section, I summarize the scientific and psychiatric viewpoints and explain why I believe the coincidences in my story have their source in another reality.

As mentioned earlier, ADCs come in three basic forms: sensory experiences, dreams, and symbolic signs. A sensory ADC involves one or more of the following senses: sight, hearing, touch, smell, or a sense of the deceased's presence. Skeptics dismiss sensory ADCs as hallucinations, dreams as nocturnal phantasms, and signs as delusions.

Skeptics make two arguments against signs and coincidences. First, human beings are hardwired to see patterns and connections because that's how we learn about the world. Sometimes, though, we see patterns and make connections where none exist, as when we see faces in the clouds or images in a Rorschach inkblot test.

Second, say the skeptics, what we think are meaningful coincidences are in fact meaningless random events, products of pure chance. For example, if you take a large enough number of random events, recognizable patterns will emerge now and then from chance alone. Given the law of large numbers, odd coincidences will occur just by accident. It's a big world, and strange things are bound to happen.

ADCs are experienced by a wide variety of people of all ages in all walks of life who seem quite ordinary and sane. Are all of them just experiencing a brief episode of mild insanity? The psychiatric profession has officially concluded that it is *not* a symptom of mental disorder for a bereaved person to have a "hallucinatory experience" and think that "he or she hears the voice of, or transiently sees the image of, the deceased person." The ADC is judged as a benign hallucination. Moreover, say the psychiatrists, "Transient hallucinatory experiences may occur in people without a mental disorder." So, if you experience a sensory ADC, you're okay.

If you have an ADC dream, it is an unusual dream, not a symptom of mental disorder. When it comes to signs, the issue is delusion, a false belief based on a misinterpretation of external reality. According to the official psychiatric view, if a person attaches "special significance" to "random events," such as coincidences, and "believes that he or she has a special message from a deity," that person may be having a delusion.

Delusion or not, it is not a symptom of mental disorder if the person's beliefs are consistent with widely held and culturally sanctioned religious or spiritual beliefs. Of course, millions of normal people do attach special significance to coincidences. If you are one of them, you're okay, too. The psychiatrists defer to public opinion. ADCs are so commonplace and therapeutic they are treated as benign. They are more than that. ADCs are divine therapy.

Symbolic signs, at least in principle and often in fact, can be verified. There may be witnesses and other proof that the sign did occur as reported. My story is an example. A number of signs have a witness in addition to me or came to people other than me. The rest of the signs come from books or texts that anyone can examine. My story can be checked and verified. You don't have to take my word for it that these things happened.

Signs require interpretation. Skeptics may say I have imposed my own explanation on random events and given them a meaning that is not there. Not true. Several signs contain ancient symbols, such as a sparrow, hawk, hawk feather, or falling star, that have established meanings, just as words in the dictionary have established meanings.

Other signs contain modern symbols that are easy to interpret, such as a church sanctuary and a minister. Finally, several signs are short sentences or phrases with obvious meanings. Why symbols? As Carol Zaleski, a Smith College professor of religion, points out, "If God, the unknowable, wishes to be known, what other recourse does God have but to avail himself of our images and symbols?"

In my story, not just one or two coincidences occur, but a whole series of them, all happening within a matter of weeks starting only days after Susan's death. Are so many coincidences of such ingenious design coming one after another in such a logical sequence just a random cluster of events? Is this symbolic allegory nothing more than a random accident of nature?

Imagine the odds of the following: A man who just lost his wife enters the sanctuary of a church accompanied by a minister. The sanctuary is empty. The wife selected "His Eye Is on the Sparrow" for her memorial service. A sparrow enters the sanctuary through a window cracked open only two inches, flies over the man's shoulder, and lights on a window in front of him. No bird is known to have been in the sanctuary before.

That's just the first sign. The odds of a series of signs happening by chance are extremely remote. To say it another way, the mathematical probability of a series of unlikely coincidences happening, and happening in a given order, all by chance, shrinks to a possibility so vanishingly small as to border on the impossible.

Statistics, however, cannot resolve the issue. Coincidences can be described as a surprising concurrence of events with no apparent causal connection. Lacking any conventional explanation or cause for a coincidence, a statistician has no choice. No matter how unlikely it is that the coincidence happened by chance, the statistician must conclude that it happened by chance nevertheless. For a series of coincidences (a super-coincidence), the conclusion is always the same: they happened by chance.

On the one hand, there are those who believe that coincidences, regardless of overwhelming odds to the contrary, are nothing more than random accidents of nature with no meaning. On the other hand, there are those who believe meaningful coincidences are never accidental, that all such coincidences are connections to an unseen reality. For them, such coincidences are God-incidences.

No doubt, some coincidences happen by chance. Some may fall in a gray area of uncertainty where you are not sure whether the coincidence happened by chance or by design. I believe the coincidences in my story happened by design. They are just too many, too perfect, and too well-orchestrated for me to attribute them to mere chance.

Psychological studies of coincidence show that when a coincidence happens to us personally, it means more to us and affects us more than it does other people. So I cannot be an objective observer of my own experience. But then scientists with pet theories often are not very objective, either.

As mentioned earlier, 20 percent of Americans, 60 million people, are estimated to have had one or more ADC experiences. Scientists are not impressed. The number of such incidents does not change their analysis or their conclusions. Scientists want empirical, reproducible evidence that can be verified by repeated observation or experiment. For scientists, ADC accounts, no matter how numerous, are only anecdotal evidence based on subjective experience.

Nevertheless, it is hard to dismiss each and every one of those millions of ADCs as products of wishful thinking, an overactive imagination, or misfires in the brain. The numbers are just too large to write them all off summarily. Something must be going on.

British biologist J. B. S. Haldane once said, "The universe is not only stranger than we imagine, it is stranger than we can imagine." Current developments in cosmology bear him out. Scientists speculate that another universe similar to ours may exist alongside ours, hovering less than a millimeter away, a parallel universe that we are unaware of because we are separated from it by a fourth spatial dimension.

Along those lines, theologian and author N. T. Wright concludes that heaven and earth intersect and are "twin interlocking spheres of God's single created reality" separated only by a "thin curtain." If so, heaven is not way out there somewhere; it is right here, right now, both immanent and transcendent. Immanent because heaven surrounds us, transcendent because it is beyond our reach.

Astronomer and author Chet Raymo writes that scientific knowledge will always be "a finite island in a sea of inexhaustible mystery." Harvard biologist Edward Wilson agrees. "Our sense of wonder grows exponentially: the greater the knowledge, the deeper the mystery," the unfathomable mystery of existence. Science is not our only way of knowing. In my heart of hearts, I believe that what happened to me was real, that the signs I experienced came from another reality, and that the messages I received are true.

The Bible and ADCs

ADCs have a biblical basis and fulfill biblical promises. They reassure us that our deceased loved ones are alive and in heaven and that death does not separate us from their love and concern for us. They reassure us that there is life after death so that we need not live in fear of death.

But first, who am I, a corporate lawyer of all things, to write about the Bible? I can only quote Martin Luther, who declared that "experience makes a theologian." And I have had a religious experience so profound that it changed my life. I write this brief theology of ADCs not only with my head but also from my heart so that you may share in my discoveries and take comfort from them.

Biblical basis

Visitations, dreams, and signs are all found in the Bible. The most famous visitations in history are the appearances of Jesus shortly after his death. But those appearances are not the only visitations reported in the Bible. For example, at the time of Jesus' transfiguration, while the disciples Peter, James, and John are watching, the ancient and long-dead prophets Moses and Elijah suddenly appear and begin talking with Jesus, a classic ADC from the New Testament.

When Jesus was on the cross, a criminal on the cross next to him said, "Jesus, remember me when you come into your kingdom." Jesus replied, "Truly I tell you, today you will be with me in paradise." So we know from the Bible that our deceased loved ones are in heaven with Jesus.

We also know from the Bible that Jesus is lord of the living and the dead. In other words, he is lord of those living in this world, and lord of those who have died and are living with him in heaven. Because he is lord, any contacts we may have from a loved one in heaven can happen only in accordance with God's will and by his grace. ADCs are a gift from God.

According to the Bible, there are different spiritual gifts, each a manifestation of the Holy Spirit. Some people are given the gift of discerning spirits. Those who experience an ADC have been given the gift, if only for the occasion, of discerning the spirit of a deceased loved one.

But how, you may ask, does one determine when an ADC comes from a heavenly source and not from a lower source? The Bible supplies a test: "By their fruit you will know them." When the fruit of an ADC is faith, hope, love, joy, peace, goodness, forgiveness, and healing, you know the ADC comes from God because those gifts are fruit of the Spirit.

Promise of comfort to those who mourn

In the Sermon on the Mount, Jesus said, "Blessed are those who mourn, for they will be comforted." ADCs bring divine comfort and healing to those who grieve. They reassure us that our deceased loved ones are alive and well and concerned about us. We are separated only for a time. Since millions of Americans are estimated to have received one or more ADCs, ADCs are a significant fulfillment of the biblical promise. For Jesus' promise to be the most effective, the comfort must come soon after the loved one's death. That explains why most ADCs occur shortly after a loved one's death.

Jurgen Moltmann, a renowned theologian, states that the comfort promised to mourners by this beatitude will be provided by the society of fellow church members and by self-help support groups of the bereaved. Those are important sources of comfort, but they are comforts of this world, unlike the heavenly rewards and compensations the beatitudes seem to envision. ADCs by comparison provide comfort from heaven itself, making them a powerful and appropriate fulfillment of the biblical promise.

Why, then, don't all mourners receive an ADC? No one knows the mind of God. However, God often works through others, just as Moltmann states. Perhaps those of us fortunate enough to receive an ADC are supposed to share our stories with others in need. In my own experience, hearing the ADC stories of others was a great comfort. Just reading ADC stories was comforting.

Promise of freedom from fear of death

Sooner or later, we will all die. Human beings are cursed with the awareness of that brutal fact. We may try to hide from it and deny it, but death is part of life. It is all around us, a constant reminder of our own fate.

Jesus came, says the Bible, to free those "held in slavery by their fear of death." He came that we "might have life, and have it more abundantly." An abundant life is problematic if we live in fear of death, a primal and existential fear. Even when repressed, that fear takes the form of a death anxiety that surfaces with age, illness, injury, pain, and suffering, and with disaster, disease, deprivation, famine, violence, and war.

Nearly two thousand years have passed since Jesus' resurrection, and many of us have difficulty believing in life after death. That's perfectly reasonable—and biblical. Even in Jesus' time, the apostle Paul had a hard time convincing some of the Corinthians who refused to believe in a resurrection of the dead. Paul cited eyewitness testimony of people still living who had seen the risen Jesus. For skeptical Corinthians, that was not good enough.

We are like the Corinthians. Numerous current examples of after-death contacts are not enough to satisfy us if the only evidence for them is someone else's testimony. We are like Thomas, who refused to believe the eyewitness testimony of his fellow disciples that they had seen the risen Jesus. We are like the Galileans of whom Jesus said, "Unless you people see miraculous signs and wonders, you will never believe."

We want direct personal experience, firsthand knowledge, before we are willing to believe (maybe) that life after death is for real. Life after death is an extraordinary claim. Extraordinary claims demand extraordinary proof. Someone else's experience is only secondhand knowledge for the rest of us.

ADCs are God's response. They are the miraculous signs providing the extraordinary proof we demand in order to believe in life after death. We are inundated with ADCs with the result that millions of us have direct personal experience that our deceased loved ones are alive and in heaven. We have only to believe our own experience.

Some may not trust their experience. They are not alone. When Jesus appeared to eleven disciples, "some doubted," reports Matthew. As Luke tells it, the disciples "were startled and frightened, thinking they saw a ghost." Even in their joy at seeing Jesus again, they were disbelieving until Jesus reassured them he was not a ghost.

I can imagine how the disciples felt. When I asked Susan to send me a sign, I also asked her not to scare me. I was afraid I could not cope with an appearance from her. It might overwhelm me, and I probably would not believe my own eyes.

Moltmann teaches that when we lose a loved one, God, because he loves us, suffers with us. In Moltmann's words, God weeps with those who weep, grieves with those who grieve. Similarly, when we weep and grieve for our loved ones in heaven, they in turn must weep and grieve to see us in pain over them.

So it is altogether fitting that so many of our loved ones in heaven have been able to contact so many of us in this world, directly and personally. The Bible tells us that death does not separate us from the love of God and Jesus. ADCs show us that death also does not separate us from the love of our loved ones in heaven, who continue to care about us and watch over us.

With ADCs in plentiful number coming from heaven to millions of people, God seems determined to make it known that there is life after death, so that even in this post-Enlightenment era of scientific materialism, we need not live in fear of death.

Near-Death Experiences and ADCs

Four percent of Americans, 12 million people, are estimated to have had a near-death experience (NDE). By comparison, 20 percent of Americans, 60 million people, are estimated to have had an ADC experience, which is five times as many as those who have had an NDE. Nevertheless, NDEs are better known than ADCs, and the research and literature on NDEs is more extensive than that for ADCs, probably because NDEs often result in dramatic personal accounts of otherworldly, out-of-body experiences, and partly because a number of NDEs take place in hospitals, attracting the attention of hospital staff.

By comparison, most ADC accounts are modest and brief. Consequently, NDEs have received a great deal more attention and publicity. They have generated at least three nonfiction best sellers, including one by a Baptist minister describing his experience. For an overview of commentary on NDEs, see Mark Fox, *Religion, Spirituality and the Near-Death Experience*. See also, Carol Zaleski, *The Life of the World to Come: Near-Death Experience and Christian Hope*.

Jerry Walls, a philosophy of religion professor at Asbury Theological Seminary, argues in *Heaven: The*

Logic of Eternal Joy that NDEs provide "at least prima facie evidence for life after death." In other words, based on the evidence provided by NDEs, one may reasonably believe that it is more probable than not that there is life after death. Professor Walls' analytical framework would seem to apply equally to ADCs. Although prima facie evidence falls well short of clear and convincing evidence, it is reassuring nevertheless.

Kenneth Ring, a prominent writer and expert on NDEs, writes in *Lessons from the Light: What we can learn from the near-death experience* that NDEs + ADCs = immense hope for those tormented with questions about the continued existence of deceased loved ones. Further, he writes, ADCs give added confidence to the testimony of so many NDErs that there is no death. People who have an ADC or near-death experience have much in common. The experience can be so powerful for an individual that for him the experience is clear and convincing evidence of life after death.

Even if a grand proof of life after death is beyond mortal reach, the huge numbers of near-death and ADC experiences provide support and validation for each individual's personal experience, reinforcing his confidence in his experience and its implications. And for some, maybe for a great many, who have not had such experiences, those many experiences are comforting and reassuring good news, inspiring hope for an afterlife.

Notes and Commentary

Introduction

God's promise of eternal life: "For God so loved the world that he gave his only son, so that whoever believes in him shall not perish but have eternal life." John 3:16.

An after-death communication (ADC) is a direct and spontaneous spiritual experience: Bill and Judy Guggenheim, *Hello from Heaven! A New Field of Research—After-Death Communication* (1995), p. 16. Their book is a seminal work, a classic in the field.

Following the Guggenheims' example, ADCs are defined to exclude any contacts that might be considered the result of an occult practice. Only ADCs as so defined are relevant to my experience and to my understanding of the religious implications of ADCs.

Other terms used for after-death communications include *afterlife encounters*, *after-death contacts*, *contact experiences*, and *visitations*.

At least 20 percent of the U.S. population is estimated to have had one or more after-death communications: Guggenheim, *Hello from Heaven!*, p. 21.

1. Before Susan's Death

All the saints in heaven: In the New Testament, "saints" are any Christians. On All Saints Day, November 1, our deceased loved ones in heaven are remembered and honored.

The two ADC books: Louis LaGrand, *After-Death Communication: Final Farewells* (1997) and *Messages and Miracles: Extraordinary Experiences of the Bereaved* (1999).

Rev. Skip Masback, the associate minister: Rev. Harold E. "Skip" Masback, III, was appointed senior minister in 2001 after Rev. Lidabell Lunt Pollard retired. A founding partner of a successful Washington, DC law firm, he left to pursue a career in the ministry. He holds degrees from Williams College, Columbia University Law School, and Yale Divinity School.

Asking Susan for a sign, praying with Skip for one: Ask your loved one while he or she is alive to send you a sign. Pray for one, too. You never know. If you do receive a sign, whether or not you asked for it or prayed for it, be sure to thank your loved one and him who made it possible. Gratitude may encourage further contacts.

2. A Sparrow

Celestial mechanics: My story is replete with coincidences, an uncanny chain of them. Carl Jung, the renowned Swiss psychoanalyst, coined the term *synchronicity* to describe meaningful coincidences. C. G. Jung, *Synchronicity: An Acausal Connecting Principle* (1973), p. 25.

Synchronistic events are symbolic, meaningful, emotional, and improbable, and they often occur at a turning point in one's life. Robert Hopcke, *There Are No Accidents: Synchronicity and the Stories of Our Lives* (1997), p. 23. They are experiences that touch the soul.

My first words when staring at the sparrow: The first words that come to mind, a free association, may give you an important clue to the meaning of a sign. Denise Linn, *The Secret Language of Signs: How to Interpret the Coincidences and Symbols in Your Life* (1996), p. 75.

Sparrow an ordinary, common bird in the Bible: It also is a Christian symbol.

Even the sparrow finds a home at the altars of God. Psalm 84:3.

"Are not two sparrows sold for a penny? Yet not a single sparrow falls to the ground without your Father knowing." Matthew 10:29.

It was this passage that inspired the words to "His Eye Is on the Sparrow," 1905, lyrics by Civilla Martin (1866–1948).

The story is told that the sparrow "was the one bird present throughout the crucifixion of Christ, making it a symbol of triumph after long-suffering." Ted Andrews, *Animal-Speak: The Spiritual & Magical Powers of Creatures Great & Small* (1993), p. 191. Similarly, the sparrow is a symbol of Susan's triumph over death after a long battle with cancer.

"Early Christians sometimes decorated their tombs with pictures of sparrows escaping from cages to illustrate the Christian soul escaping the prison of this life and flying to heaven." Suzetta Tucker, *Christian Legends & Symbols—The Bestiary—Sparrow* (1999), an Internet e-text.

Sparrows are part of an early Christian tale about Jesus as a child. When Jesus was five years old, he and some other children were playing by the waters of a brook. It was the Sabbath.

Jesus made some soft mud, and from it fashioned twelve sparrows. When a certain Jew saw what Jesus had done, he promptly reported it to his father, Joseph, complaining that Jesus had profaned the Sabbath.

When Joseph arrived at the scene and saw what had happened, he reprimanded his son for breaking the Sabbath. Undaunted, Jesus clapped his hands and cried out to the sparrows, "Be gone!" And the sparrows took off, chirping. *The Infancy Gospel of Thomas* 2:1–5 in Bart Ehrman, *Lost Scriptures: Books that Did Not Make It into the New Testament* (2003), p. 58.

One book leaps off the page: S. Sparrow, *I Am With You Always: True Stories of Encounters with Jesus* (1995), contemporary accounts of visitations by Jesus in visions and dreams. This book is on a suggested reading list in LaGrand, *Messages and Miracles*, p. 302.

After his resurrection, Jesus' last words to his disciples, as recorded in Matthew 28:20, were "Lo, I am with you always, even to the end of the age."

3. Another Sparrow

My spelling error: for *sings* I mistakenly write *signs*, an anagram of *sings*. Seemingly random mistakes that occur in life can be signs in disguise. Linn, *The Secret Language of Signs*, p. 48.

4. A Fireball

A fireball: The American Meteor Society has a Fireball Monitoring Program. Rarely are shooting stars fireballs. amsmeteors.org.

5. A Hawk

The hawk was beautiful and graceful: Later, I realize that *graceful* also means "full of grace," as befits a messenger from God.

Sandy's book: Native Americans in Southern California "believed that hawks were messengers of the Great Spirit, and that if a hawk landed near you, it meant that God had a message for you." Thomas and Penelope Pauley, *I'm Rich Beyond My Wildest Dreams* (1999), pp. 1–2.

"The sky is the realm of the hawk. Through its flight it communicates with humans and with the great creator spirit." Andrews, *Animal-Speak*, p. 155.

God announcing his presence: Shooting stars were regarded as a divine manifestation or as a message from heaven. Jean Chevalier and Alain Gheerbrant, *Penguin Dictionary of Symbols*, 2nd edition (1982), p. 878.

In ancient times, people often believed falling stars were divine missives or omens, a warning or announcement that presaged important events. Patricia Telesco, *The Language of Dreams* (1997), pp. 182, 247. For me, it was the coming of the hawk.

The red-tailed hawk is a messenger: To the Sioux, it is known as red hawk. Ed McGaa, Eagle Man, *Mother Earth Spirituality* (1990), pp. 161, 178–79. To the Pueblo, it was known as red eagle. Andrews, *Animal-Speak*, p. 155.

6. A Hawk Feather

I found this hawk feather, and I want you to have it: "Finding a feather can signify an important message from the Creator." Linn, *The Secret Language of Signs*, p. 151.

You will be given feathers by others "who may not know why they are giving you such a present but only that it feels right for you." Andrews, *Animal-Speak*, p. 69. See also Maril Crabtree, *Sacred Feathers: The Power of One Feather to Change Your Life* (2002).

10. Follow Your Bliss

One book stands out: Hal Bennett and Susan Sparrow, *Follow Your Bliss* (1997).

Carl Jung received an ADC where only the title of a book, not the content, was significant. C. G. Jung, *Memories, Dreams, Reflections* (1973), p. 313. For me, only the coauthor's name, the title, and the cover are significant.

11. A Third Hawk, a Third Sparrow

The words of Jesus spoken to me: When I turned on the car radio, I happened to catch the minister who was speaking at the exact moment he uttered the words "I am with you always." Matthew 28:20. Another coincidence.

The special significance for the Sioux of a red-tailed hawk: McGaa, *Mother Earth Spirituality*, pp. 161–63.

Sioux = Sue: Homophones are words such as *night* and *knight*, or *great* and *grate*, that are pronounced the same but differ in meaning and spelling. Sometimes signs appear in life as homophones. Linn, *The Secret Language of Signs*, p. 51.

A red-tailed hawk, my own "Sue" messenger: The red-tailed hawk stimulates hope and new ideas. "It reflects a need to be open to the new or shows you ways that you may help teach others to be open to the new." Andrews, *Animal-Speak*, pp. 154–55.

12. A Glimpse of God's Glory

The valley of the shadow of death: Psalm 23.

Those who mourn will be comforted: Matthew 5:4. I am indebted to Rev. Masback for his observation that ADCs fulfill the biblical promise.

A numinous experience: Rudolf Otto, a German theologian, coined the term *numinous* to describe the deeply felt experience of an encounter with the Divine. The different feelings one can have from such an encounter range from the terrifying to the sublime. Otto, *The Idea of the Holy*, 2nd edition (1950). It's an experience where one feels "undeniably, irresistibly, and unforgettably in the presence of the Divine." Hopcke, *There Are No Accidents*, p. 30.

If Jesus was not raised, our faith is futile: 1 Corinthians 15:17–19.

Hundreds of accounts of modern-day ADC experiences: See the books listed under Further Reading.

All-powerful, all-knowing, ever-present, all-loving: In scholarly terms—omnipotent, omniscient, omnipresent, omnibenevolent. God is all-loving because God *is* love. 1 John 4:8, 16

Science and Coincidence

Science and Coincidence: John Allen Paulos, *Innumeracy: Mathematical Illiteracy and Its Consequences* (1988), chap. 2 "Probability and Coincidence," p. 33. Jill Neimark, "Pattern & Circumstance: The Power of Coincidence," *Psychology Today*, July/Aug. 2004, p. 47. Lisa Belkin, "The Odds of That: Coincidence in an Age of Conspiracy," *New York Times Magazine*, Aug. 11, 2002, p. 32.

ADCs are *not* symptoms of mental disorder: American Psychiatric Association, *Diagnostic and Statistical Manual of Mental Disorders*, 4th edition (1994) (known as the DSM-IV), pp. 296–99, 684–85, 765, 767.

God availing himself of our images and symbols: Carol Zaleski, *The Life of the World to Come: Near-Death Experience and Christian Hope* (1996), p. 35.

Scientists speculate on cosmos: For a survey of theories, see Brian Greene, *The Fabric of the Cosmos* (2004); Michio Kaku, *Parallel Worlds* (2005); and Lisa Randall, *Warped Passages: Unraveling the Mysteries of the Universe's Hidden Dimensions* (2005). Beware: these books are not easy reading.

Heaven and earth intersect and are separated only by a thin curtain: N. T. Wright, *Surprised by Hope: Rethinking Heaven, the Resurrection, and the Mission of the Church* (2008), pp. 250–52.

Scientific knowledge a finite island in a sea of inexhaustible mystery: Chet Raymo, *Skeptics and True Believers: The Exhilarating Connection Between Science and Religion* (1998), p. 48.

Our sense of wonder grows exponentially: Edward Wilson, *Biophilia* (1984), p. 10.

The Bible and ADCs

Martin Luther (1483–1546): a German theologian who launched the Protestant Reformation (1517–1648).

Experience makes a theologian: as quoted in Alister McGrath, *Christian Theology: an Introduction*, 3rd edition (2001), p. 191.

Biblical basis

Moses and Elijah appear and talk with Jesus: Mark 9:2–4.

Today you will be with me in paradise: Luke 23:42–43.

Christ is lord of the living and the dead: Romans 14:9.

Gift of discerning spirits: 1 Corinthians 12:10.

By their fruit you will know them: Matthew 7:16.

Fruit of the Spirit: 1 Corinthians 12:9, 13:13, Galatians 5:22.

Promise of comfort to those who mourn

Those who mourn will be comforted: Matthew 5:4.

Comfort for mourners to come from church members and self-help groups: Jurgen Moltmann, *The Coming of God: Christian Eschatology* (1996), p. 127.

Beatitudes: The declarations of blessedness pronounced by Jesus in the Sermon on the Mount. Matthew 5:3–11.

Promise of freedom from fear of death

Jesus came to free those held in slavery by their fear of death: Hebrews 2:15.

He came that we might have life more abundantly: John 10:10.

Corinthians disbelieve in resurrection of dead: 1 Corinthians 15.

Thomas doubts Jesus' resurrection: John 20:24–28.

Galileans need miraculous signs and wonders to believe: John 4:48.

Jesus appears to eleven disciples, some doubt: Matthew 28:16–17.

Disciples see Jesus and think they see a ghost: Luke 24:36–43.

God suffers with us: Moltmann, *The Coming of God*, p. 126.

Death not a separation from love of God and Jesus: Romans 8:38–39.

Near-Death Experiences and ADCs

Four percent of Americans are estimated to have had a near-death experience: Guggenheim, *Hello from Heaven!*, p. 21.

At least 20 percent of Americans are estimated to have had an ADC experience: Guggenheim, above, p. 21.

Three NDE non-fiction best sellers: Raymond Moody, *Life after Life* (1975); Betty Eadie, *Embraced by the Light* (1992); Don Piper, *90 Minutes in Heaven* (2004). Mr. Piper is a Baptist minister.

NDEs are prima facie evidence for life after death: Jerry Walls, *Heaven: The Logic of Eternal Joy* (2002), p. 160.

NDEs + ADCs = immense hope: Kenneth Ring, *Lessons from the Light: What we can learn from the near-death experience* (1998), p. 269.

Later printings or editions of works cited above may have made changes in the cover, the text or the pagination. Also, any Web site or Internet content mentioned herein may change or cease to exist.

Further Reading

After-Death Communications

Arcangel, Dianne. *Afterlife Encounters: Ordinary People, Extraordinary Experiences*. Charlottesville, VA: Hampton Roads, 2005.

Browning, Sinclair. *Feathers Brush My Heart: True Stories of Mothers Connecting With Their Daughters After Death*. New York: Grand Central Publishing, 2002.

Devers, Edie. *Goodbye Again: Experiences with Departed Loved Ones*. Kansas City, MO: Andrews & McMeel, 1997.

Duminiak, Christine. *God's Gift of Love: After-Death Communications—For Those Who Grieve*. Charleston, SC: BookSurge, 2003.

Finley, Mitch. *Whispers of Love: Inspiring Encounters with Deceased Relatives and Friends*. New York: Crossroad, 1995.

Greer, Jane. *The Afterlife Connection*. New York: St. Martin's, 2003.

Guggenheim, Bill & Guggenheim, Judy. *Hello from Heaven! A New Field of Research—After-Death Communication*. New York: Bantam, 1995.

LaGrand, Louis. *Love Lives On: Learning from the Extraordinary Encounters of the Bereaved*. New York: Penguin, 2006.

———. *Messages and Miracles: Extraordinary Experiences of the Bereaved*. St. Paul, MN: Llewellyn, 1999. Answers to the 100 most-asked questions about ADCs.

———. *After-Death Communication: Final Farewells*. St. Paul, MN: Llewellyn, 1997.

Lawson, Lee. *Visitations from the Afterlife: True Stories of Love and Healing*. San Francisco: HarperCollins, 2000.

Lewis, C.S. *A Grief Observed*. New York: HarperCollins, 1961.

Martin, Joel & Romanowski, Patricia. *Love Beyond Life: The Healing Power of After-Death Communications*. New York: HarperCollins, 1997.

Wright, Sylvia. *When Spirits Come Calling: The Open-Minded Skeptic's Guide to After-Death Contacts*. Nevada City, CA: Blue Dolphin, 2002.

Synchronicity/Coincidence

Cousineau, Phil. *Soul Moments: Marvelous Stories of Synchronicity—Meaningful Coincidences from a*

Seemingly Random World. Berkeley, CA: Conari, 1997. Also titled *Coincidence or Destiny?*

Halberstam, Yitta & Levanthal, Judith. *Small Miracles: Extraordinary Coincidences from Everyday Life.* Holbrook, MA: Adams Media, 1997. First in a series of *Small Miracles* books, each a collection of stories of remarkable coincidences.

Hopcke, Robert. *There Are No Accidents: Synchronicity and the Stories of Our Lives.* New York: Penguin, 1997.

Jung, C.G. *Synchronicity: An Acausal Connecting Principle.* Princeton, NJ: Princeton University Press, 1973.

Plimmer, Martin & King, Brian. *Beyond Coincidence: Stories of Amazing Coincidences and the Mystery and Mathematics Behind Them.* New York: St. Martin's, 2006.

Rushnell, Squire. *When God Winks at You: How God Speaks Directly to You Through the Power of Coincidence.* Nashville, TN: Thomas Nelson, 2006.

Wheeler, Karla. *Afterglow: Signs of Continued Love—Stories of Comforting Coincidences from Those Who Grieve.* Naples, FL: Quality of Life Publishing, 2002.

Heaven

Alcorn, Randy. *Heaven.* Wheaton, IL: Tyndale House, 2004.

DeStefano, Anthony. *A Travel Guide to Heaven*. New York: Doubleday, 2003.

Kreeft, Peter. *Everything You Ever Wanted to Know about Heaven But Never Dreamed of Asking*. San Francisco: Ignatius Press, 1990.

MacArthur, John. *The Glory of Heaven: The Truth About Heaven, Angels and Eternal Life*. Wheaton, IL: Good News Publishers, 1996.

McDannell, Colleen & Lang, Bernhard. *Heaven: A History*. 2nd ed. New Haven, CT: Yale University Press, 2001.

McGrath, Alister. *A Brief History of Heaven*. Oxford, UK: Blackwell Publishing, 2003.

Roberts, Arthur. *Exploring Heaven: What Great Christian Thinkers Tell Us About Our Afterlife with God*. New York: HarperCollins, 2003.

About the Author

Morey McDaniel is a retired corporate lawyer. For twenty years, he was chief finance counsel in the law department of a large industrial corporation headquartered in New York City, and later in Connecticut. Before that, he was with a Wall Street law firm in New York City. He is the author of several articles in professional law journals.

Morey was born and grew up in Springfield, Missouri. He graduated from Wesleyan University with high honors and was elected to Phi Beta Kappa, a national honor society. He earned his law degree from Stanford Law School and an advanced law degree from Harvard Law School.

Susan, his wife of thirty-nine years, died in July 2000 from cancer. Shortly after her death, Morey and several others received a number of extraordinary signs and messages from Susan that changed his life and led to this, his first book.

A resident of New Canaan, Connecticut, for many years, Morey again lives in his hometown, Springfield, Missouri.